SNOOKER

THE GOLDEN RULES OF SNOOKER

A CORGI BOOK 0 552 12599 7

First publication in Great Britain

PRINTING HISTORY
Corgi edition published 1985

Corgi Books are published by Transworld Publishers Ltd.,
Century House, 61-63 Uxbridge Road, Ealing, London W5 5SA,
in Australia by Transworld Publishers (Aust.) Pty. Ltd.,
26 Harley Crescent, Condell Park, NSW 2200, and in New
Zealand by Transworld Publishers (N.Z.) Ltd., Cnr. Moselle
and Waipareira Avenues, Henderson, Auckland.

Made and printed in Great Britain by
Hunt Barnard Printing Ltd., Aylesbury, Bucks.

A Player should choose a cue with great care, and ensure that it is strong.

At all times when playing a shot, one foot must be in contact with the ground.

It is essential for the serious Player to practise when and wherever possible.

The Player should be well-balanced when playing a shot.

The triangle must be removed before a Player breaks.

It is permissible for a Player to use a screw-in extension to his cue.

Clothes should be comfortable and not tight-fitting.

The right arm should be the only part of the body that moves while making a shot.

The Player may not touch any ball or balls on the table with any part of his body.

An Opponent must not annoy or distract the Player.

A cue shall be not less than three feet in length and shall show no substantial departure from the traditional and generally accepted shape and form.

The Referee will penalize a Player for consistent time-wasting.

If a Player is colour-blind, the Referee shall tell him the colour of a ball if requested.

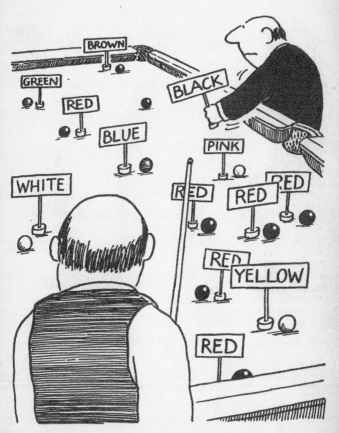

For conduct which, in the opinion of the Referee, is wilfully or persistently unfair, a Player shall lose the game, and is liable to be disqualified from any future competition.

A Player may not bang or cause vibrations to the table in order to pocket a ball to his advantage or for any other reason.

In a Championship, the table must be thoroughly brushed and ironed before each match.

For playing improperly from the 'D', the penalty is the value of the 'on' ball, or of the ball struck, or of the ball pocketed, whichever is the greatest.

The Referee will stand in a position where he can best see clearly the play.

The Jump Shot is a foul in which the cue-ball is made to jump over any ball whether by accident or design.

Two balls must not be struck simultaneously.

For playing the ball with anything but the cue, the penalty is the value of the 'on' ball, or of the ball touched, whichever is greater.

The Player must be fairly fit before playing in a match or an important game.

The Referee's decision is final, and a Player must not dispute his judgement.

Only the Referee is allowed to clean a ball on the table, and then only at the request of a Player.

Cigarettes, drinks or any other articles must not be left on the edge of the table.

In some Tournaments or Championships it may be necessary for the Player to wear a tie.

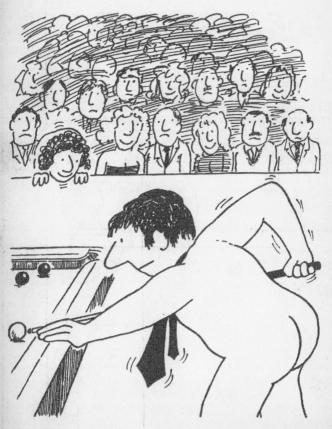

During a frame the Referee is the only person allowed to handle a ball.

The Player may not receive advice whilst a match is in progress.

The rest must not be left on the table.

The Non-Striker shall, when the Striker is playing, sit or stand at a fair distance from the table.

The Screw is an important, and often necessary, shot in the game and must be practised to perfection.

The Player should ignore any comments or remarks from spectators.

A Non-Striker, or Non-Player, shall not cause the Striker to touch or move a ball.

A ball is 'forced off the table' which comes to rest otherwise than on the bed of the table or in a pocket. This is a foul shot.

When requested by the Referee, a Player must state which ball he is 'on'.

The Referee shall not give any advice or express opinion on points affecting play.

To use spin to advantage a Player will need to practise this particular shot for many hours.

The table must not be moved or tilted by a Player during a frame.

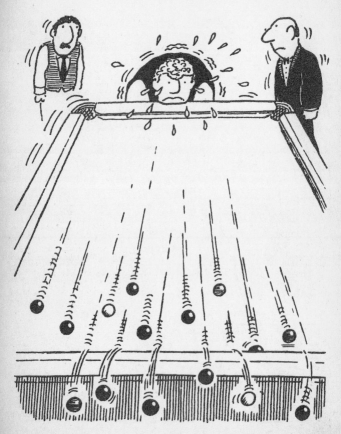

The cue-ball must be hit with the tip of the cue.

It is important to remain calm and as relaxed as possible during a match, as stress and tension will only cause mistakes.

Great care must be taken when playing the cue-ball which is resting on the cushion, as this is one of the trickiest shots of the game.

The Player must practise the Stun Shot, as this will usually be needed at some point in a frame.

The Referee should not give any indication that a Player is about to make a foul stroke.

Always be graceful in defeat.

The Marker shall keep the score on the marking board, and assist the Referee to carry out his duties.